# JOY//US

## Poems of Queer Joy

Edited by

Cherry Potts

and

Jeremy Dixon

First published in UK 2024 by Arachne Press Limited
100 Grierson Road, London SE23 1NX
www.arachnepress.com

ISBNs
Print 978-1-913665-89-0
eBook 978-1-913665-90-6



Thanks to Muireann Grealy, for her proofing.

Printed on woodfree paper in the UK.

**With huge thanks to our crowdfund supporters,**
**Kythé Beaumont, Mark Senior and Poetry Pharmacy,**
**and the 60 other individual supporters**
**who helped bring this book to fruition.**

Acknowledgements

Introduction © Cherry Potts & Jeremy Dixon 2024
*A Night in t'Pub* © Joshua Linney 2024
*Abracadabra!* and *Small Green Thing* © John McCullough 2024
*After the Parade* and *Heading Out* © Aoife Mannix 2024
*Balcony Scene* © Rick Dove 2024
*Blessed Be* and *Hip Hop Line Dancing in Dallas* © Dean Atta 2024
*Bread the Love* © Abhi 2024
*Coming-home Jeans* © Elizabeth Gibson 2024
*Dance Free on Hope* and *Great Queen Street* © Cherry Potts 2024
*Dirty Dykes* and *Them and They* © Vron McIntyre 2024
*does it fit* © Conway Emmett
*Don't* © Joy Howard 2024
*First* © Laurie B. 2024
*First Night, New Town* © Sophia Blackwell 2024
*Flexible* © Mwelwa Chilekwa 2024
*Flint Knapping is Queer Now* © K. Angel 2024
*Foundation* © Desree 2024
*Fresh* © Kate Foley 2024
*Gorse Track* and *Women, Lava* © Maria Jastrzębska 2024
*Her Blue Shirt* © Annie Kerr 2024
*How We Love* © Khakan Qureshi, BEM 2024
*In a Meadow a Girl Holds her Friend's Hand* © Elizabeth Chadwick Pywell 2024
*Instead of a Bible* and *Onion* © Lydia Fulleylove 2024
*JOY//US* and *While Cruising Cardiff Bay* © Jeremy Dixon 2024
*Legacy* © Steph Morris 2024
*Living* © Lawrence Wilson 2024
*Madison Square Park on July 14th* © Robert Hamberger 2024
*Making Queer Friends on Purpose* © Tanya Erin Sheehan 2024
*Moon* © Becky Brookfield 2024
*Old Flip-Phone Videos* © Jane Aldous 2024
*Plas Newydd* © Tom McLaughlin 2024
*Probably Won't Be a Church Service* © Rab Green 2024
*She Said Everyone Falls a Little Bit in Love With Their Friends Sometimes* © Helen Bowie 2024

# JOY//US

Contents

## Introduction
## Cherry Potts and Jeremy Dixon

Welcome to JOY//US: Poems of Queer Joy!
Arachne Press is a long-time champion of LGBTQ+ writers, in particular poets. With many collections published over the years, we decided it was time to give an opportunity to as many LGBTQ+ poets as possible, so we are delighted to present our first anthology of LGBTQ+ poetry.
These are poems that celebrate all that is wonderful about our community and communities and our individually gorgeous unique lives. This is a book for us, a book that all LGBTQ+ readers can open at random, and find a moment of poetic queer joy for themselves, however big or small.
How do we define queer joy? We have become used to seeing and hearing the phrase used in so many adverts and books and places and productions but when you really dig down, what does queer joy actually mean? What are the specifics? How do we express it? How do we measure it? (Can it be measured?) Where is queer joy found? Who gives us queer joy? And most importantly, how do you write a poem of queer joy? We don't aim to answer that in this introduction, we'll leave it for the poets as the poems in this book investigate various themes such as love, pride, nature, pop culture, food, identity, dancing and more.
We gave poets an eight-month submission period because from early exploration last January, we found that there weren't many joyful queer poems being written. Time was needed for the poets to find their way into the subject and make it their own. As we received almost a third of all

submissions in the final week, we think this plan was justified! During the submission period Jeremy ran poetry workshops both online and in bookshops around the UK (big thanks to Typewronger Books in Edinburgh, Juno Books in Sheffield, Good Bookshop in Bristol, Round Table Books in London and the pop-up Pride House in Liverpool).
What became apparent during these workshops is that many LGBTQ+ poets find it hard to write about joy. If we write about queer joy are we taking creative energy away from the more difficult and traumatic aspects of our lives that also need documenting? We received many poems which dwelt on anguish and only finished in joy, often in the final line, as though somehow joy must be earned through trauma. We received many more about pride and defiance, metaphorically sticking two fingures up to the world. Not exactly joy, though veering towards it, perhaps. While we recognise that need to show defiance fighting our way out of trauma, we also all need the joy to resource and enliven the dialogue we have with all our experiences.
We want this anthology to be a catalyst for many more poems of queer joy to leap from many more creative queer minds, and to remind us all that no matter what the world throws at us, we are very good at looking after our own, and we really know how to have fun.

**K. Angel**
**Flint Knapping Is Queer Now**

These days I carry a rock in my pocket
that I found with you that day we walked
from Margate all the way around that hump
of worn coastline that former island
those beaches and cliffs we settled ourselves
into gradually debating the name and
properties of the black shingle that tried all
our tiniest forgotten muscles.

I wanted to believe it igneous poured
from some deep molten core long before
the Vikings or the pirates took their shelter
but you couldn't trace a history
of volcanoes not here you were right.

There is some longer poem that does justice
to these layers we've laid down or
let lie down upon us but right now I only
have the mind to awe at how we strike
each other make useful edges of the selves
we cleave how you press your thumb
to my smooth inner surfaces now exposed
help me to warm them.

**Dean Atta**
**Blessed Be**

Blessed be Black queers
in African prints and rainbow trim.
Blessed be Sunday mornings
at church with the shimmer of
Saturday night in the corners of our eyes.

Blessed be box braids on boys
and buzz cuts on girls.
Blessed be afros and dreadlocks
for all who want them.
No white hands
reaching out to touch them.

Blessed be gender-affirming and -nonconforming
hairstyles and clothing.
Blessed be our culture on our bodies,
our hairstyles on our heads,
our music on our hips, patois
and vernaculars on our lips.

Blessed be James Baldwin and Lil Nas X.
Blessed be Topher Campbell and Ajamu X.
Blessed be Big Freedia and Jean-Michel Basquiat.

Blessed be drag kings, queens and all in-between.
Blessed be Stud Life, Moonlight and Noah's Arc.
Blessed be Black queer art.

**JP Seabright**
**Short Back and Sides**

Glory to the cordless hair trimmer,
the wet shave cutthroat razor and the duster brush.

Praise be the clippers, the scissors,
and the number one all over.

All hail the bleach blonde dye, the majestic fade.
Colour me glorious, colour me curious, colour me queer.

Salutations to the snip snip buzz of the barber shop,
the low murmur of lives shared, weather dismissed,
politics discussed.

(Or is it weather discussed and politics dismissed?)

Less of *where are you going on your holidays?*
More of *where are you going to pull tonight?*

Endless gratitude for getting the look just right
for the coming adventure, to dance and dazzle
in the disco lights.

*Yeah I know the place, my boyfriend works behind the bar.*
No social pretence for our 'pretended family relationships'
We can bare it all here in the barber's chair.

Joy upon joy upon relief and release upon joy
at finding someone who understands.

The holy therapeutic hair wash, the brush down, the placing
of your life, your look, your history and identity
into another's careful hands.

**Zo Copeland**

## Trees Like Us

And I know you're still talking
As I stare off into the distance
I hear the staccato of your voice
It continues on over the breeze
But I am lost in the distance
Where a copper beech and a sycamore
The same giant height, have grown as one
Two organisms, one entity
Half and half; one side purple, one side deep green
Separate in their union
Like us
I know you're still talking
I don't hear your words
But I know what you're saying

**Rick Dove**
**Balcony Scene**

A light indignity of twos on a Marlboro,
above the city, great familiarities and something
conspiratorial, crushed in hushed tones between these
muffled beats, how oxidation and respiration mean
*We are all a multitude of tiny fires, burning*
*imperceptibly slowly* until ends in the dark,
And against it, how people come alive in low light
outside, away from the party, searching for something,
when the shadows come to dance, in the flickering
of hushed breaths flirting with a mastery.

And suddenly, our platonic nature is dancing shapes
upon a wall, a projection of reality, and my turn to speak
is a memory telling tall tales of a lost summer,
and *Mikey's grow house going up like an inferno,*
and up in this smoke *how high we got by the light*
*of that fire*, how floating embers are we,
glowing potentials to be new golden seats, sparks
caught upon the breeze, settling to be divine mischief,
a comedy of something running wild and free,
for our world is a tinderbox tight and heaving,
and these tales teach of a heat in the fuzzy edges
rubbing, the warmth in proximity, of accidental intimacy,
of a light indignity, of twos on a Marlboro
          and blow

**John McCullough**
**Small Green Thing**

I'm going to be a leaf today.
I shall fall all over the place
in decorative fashion, the wind posting me
haphazardly through slots in the air.
So much will be possible in my covert laboratory.
I shall invent outlandish rituals,
new ways of being flat and important.
I shall write *Diary of a Modern Leaf*,
describing my thrashing about in vibrant prose.
I shall swoop and ascend, startled
by my own patterns, how I keep pointing
like a signpost toward delight
which, lost so long, turned up again,
stupid, beautiful and forgiven, like the sun.

**Mwelwa Chilekwa**
**Flexible**

Like a liquid
You cannot contain me
Sure, I'll fit whatever mould
You put me in
Okay, I'll be British
But only for the time being
And for my benefit, not yours
Who I am still leaks through
Seeping through the cracks
You tape it shut but
I persevere
Who's the one really in control here?
Yes, I'm dating a man
Not because you've contained me
But due to my own will
Still the truth lies
I am bi
Try as you might
You cannot chain me
I'm as flexible as can be
I welcome you
To waste your time

**Joshua Jones**
**The Wrestler**
*after the sculpture by Henri Gaudier-Brzeska*

Place your cock
Against my cock

Ready your battle stance
Elbows crooked, palms cupped

Deliver to you, my body
Balls squeezed tight in metal

A conductor of heat, our warmth
Pressed together until collar bones pop

I am cracked. I am waiting to
Be cracked further. Bent apart and hammered

The spaces between your fingers do not fit
Mine. How can we get a grip. There's so

Much oil, bronzed skin. Sweat. This light looks good
On you. Youth in plaster cast. Death's spiral tastes

Like a mouth full of coins, a very public socking
reach for each other, again. Towel your hands and try.

**Rab Green**
## Probably Won't be a Church Service

Between aisles at the top of the supermarket, near the meat counter,
I thought
about what I'd leave behind when I die, what would be said at my
funeral,
my accomplishments all summed up:

*He, Sex.*

And I thought the sucker punch of clarity would hit me in the gut,
sad panicked
wasteful regret.
But no, not at all, sounds good.

**Tanya Erin Sheehan**
**Making Queer Friends on Purpose**

We crash through the hedgerow
Glittering fangs and twisted horns, our tails interlocked
Vegetarians who will 100% do a murder
Full of fizz and pitch-bright screams

If a man approaches
We'll run at him, laughing
'This isn't for you.
This isn't about you.
This isn't for you!'

Sure, later he'll tell everyone that
he saw some women in the woods
probably naked

But we'll forget him

We're not scary
But you should be terrified

**Vron McIntyre**

## Them and They

*after Bill, Bill, and Phil*

Shall I address thee now as 'she' or 'they'?
I undertake the mental shift required
to change what I habitually say,
and cast away old notions now expired.

Take heart in pride, thy countenance divine
as fools with old-style attitudes deride
and find a way for thy true sun to shine
while joy wells up from somewhere deep inside.

Let's live our lives as who we really are.
Respect is handed on from self to self,
truth and autonomy our guiding stars.
Euphoria deepens like a coastal shelf

Next time they ask you to, say 'them' and 'they'
and watch them blossom like a summer's day.

**Cherry Potts**
## Great Queen Street

I meet Greta Garbo in
the ladies in that ex-mission hall
on Great Queen Street where
the lesbian archive used to be,
sometime in the late 80s
after a deluged lesbian strength
march.
Me in trilby,  pinstripe suit,
she in soft brown velvet
breeches, jerkin, pirate boots
too wet for the after party
or the tube home.
*Queen Christina*, I say,
admiring. She, less certain –
*Al Capone?*
*Silvia Scarlet,* I reply
and we take off our clothes
and dry them piece by piece
under the single too-hot hand-drier.
It takes an age, shivering in
damp underwear
with Greta Garbo.
My trilby is never the same again.

**Alexander Williams**
**The Quick Camp Laugh**

tumbles from the mouth like an involuntary volcanic eruption
a powerful, rolling, physical mass of diaphragmatic production
a joyous and glorious, high-pitched, voluminous, razor-like blast of emotion
inviting affection, respect or defection, love/hate, amazement, devotion.

**Helen Bowie**
**She Said Everyone Falls a Little Bit in Love With Their Friends Sometimes**

You said I always liked talking to you and I said you too and then added a third party to a WhatsApp group because it was gone 11pm and my phone was already telling me about screen time in hours, minutes, seconds / You said it's called bi-fi and we communicate by falling in love with each other don't we and I said ha, yes and then I screenshot that and I wasn't sure why / You said something about a spider and I said something about a web and it could have been a metaphor but it wasn't and you were scared and I was not / You said you could only drink corner shop sauvignon blanc if you were drowning sorrows and I said we were getting dangerously close to real talk / You said that I was the best person ever and I said oh sorry excuse me please because I needed to get back to my seat and I don't think I was meant to hear any of what was said but I was carrying three pint glasses and a bag of Taytos and everyone knows that if you're carrying three pint glasses and a bag of Taytos you have right of way, even in conversation / You said it seemed like a long walk and I said it really wasn't that far and we could walk together / You said you didn't want to hear a poem from a drunk man on the street and I said that I did want to hear a poem from a drunk man on the street but not if I had to hear it alone / You said you'd written a story and could I read it and I said I'd love to and I should find something to send you but everything I wrote felt too emotionally honest so I found an old link to an old piece about old feelings and hit send and then I switched off my phone and went out to sea / You said you were seeing someone and I said that's great what's their name / You said that in a zombie apocalypse you would just let them get you and I said same / You said god no when a stranger on the street asked if we were in love and I said am I so hideous and I hoped it sounded like a joke even though I wasn't sure if it was / You asked me to read something else you had written and I said thank you for trusting me with this and overthought the shift from best person you know to beta reader and then I read it and I left questions marks on all of my comments even though we both knew that they were statements / You said that you were going to get a tattoo of something I said and I said I was going to get a tattoo of something I'd seen scrawled in lipstick on a toilet door / You said if it was going to happen then tonight would have been the night and I laughed.

**Tom McLaughin**
**Plas Newydd**
*for the Ladies of Llangollen*

Permit yourself to brush the edge of something
soft and yielding. Flickering halflight allows
things to become both true and half-true – things we
            could not countenance

in the morning's unforgiving glare. That space
of light and shadow must be held. *And what price*
*Rousseau by candlelight with my one true love?*
            Nine pounds a year, dear.

Speak to us now and always, plainly, freely,
of bodies cradled by twilight, of questing
hands clutching among the ferns and in the dirt,
            of torn and soiled clothes,

of rising blood in cheeks and silent chambers
crowded with books and a small marital bed
and searing looks exchanged in private studies
            that bloom into words,

of the spaces that engender and endure.
How can we hope to separate the rolling
hills from your rolling sentences, the valleys'
            contours from your days'?

Your libraries from the atriums we found
carved out for us, knowing you meditated
among your volumes in hushed union and dreamed
us into being?

**Conway Emmett**
**does it fit**

does your gender feel tactile like
the raised pattern on the
metal handle of your
favourite spoon

does it calm you like
the downstrokes and
cross-strokes of your
favourite number

does it thrill you like
the beautifully laid out rows
and columns of data in a
well-designed spreadsheet

does it harmonise like
putting your face in your
partner's bowl of strawberries
breathing inward him and them

does it warm you up like
the blanket crocheted for you
with *fucks* all over so you
don't have to give any

**Joshua Linney**
**A Night in t'Pub**

In t'dim glow of pub, we clock each other.
Barnsley lad, this ain't summat y'plan.
A shoot him a wink, our 'ands are like metal to magnet,
Jumpin abowt where only us two matter.

He's mi fella in this 'ere square foot,
Not a bit of mardy 'bout me, nah, it's electric.
Feet 'avin' their own bit on t'floor,
Shadows mixin' under that flickerin' bulb.

Ar lips meet up, nice en soft,
This 'ere moment, better than owt, feels like 'ome.

**Abhi**
**Bread the Love**

From munching on the hard crust
of your cold pizza,
to eating the burnt slices
of our sourdough,
and serving you on a platter
but eating out the packet –
sure I love you,
but I love food.
And if I haven't already said
I fucking love bread.

**Maria Jastrzębska**
**Women, Lava**

When I was your age
I had no idea
two women might
take turns
to hold their child
without hesitation
instead of in a manger
a baby could be
born on a bed of black sand
among sweet tabaiba and cacti
lizards and crabs peeking out
at its crib three crowned hoopoes
weaving not far above
no idea that in the lava's blood
where a glinting edge
of scabrous rock
has long cooled
shapes of flames
can be seen
or invented

**Steph Morris**
**Legacy**

Early days, and I found we were sitting out
on the street in the sun with a coffee,
holding hands, my love in pyjamas still,
alongside marigolds in pots,

and I found myself introducing him to the fellow
next door. On escalators I stand on the step
below, so we can kiss. We can't not.
They all look anyway.

We cuddled all down the East London Line once.
At New Cross, as we climbed the steep side street,
holding hands, this woman shouted, *you two*
*are lovely.* One year on, and the fellow

next door had a boyfriend too – still does,
and down the street there's been knock-on love.

**Robert Hamberger**
**Madison Square Park on July 14th**

A shaven-haired man in a blue T-shirt talks to the phone in his ear: *Well a poem is* – he weaves fast through dawdling people, so I can't hear the rest. What's a poem – will I ever catch it? Sparrows flurry belly-feathers in the dust. A hippy-ish woman comes to my bench and asks *Sir, do you have any pain in your body?* I say *No, I'm lucky* and her younger male companion, bearded like Jesus, smiles and says *A surprising number of people have no pain today*. It's my last afternoon in New York. I must read more Frank O'Hara. As it's gone three, Frank would have finished his lunch by now and strolled back to the gallery. The fountain splashes into three black metal basins. It settles and never settles, pouring endlessly in the sun. Each spurt of water looks white this afternoon, sprinkling against scaffolding and three black basins, palm leaves drenched in pots so they're the lushest green, drinking whatever the fountain needs to give.

**P Burton-Morgan**
**When I am Twelve a New Girl Joins Our School**

tall girl
  with caramel hair
will you be my friend?

and then
  when childhood ends
will you drink malibu in my room
            talking of boys
while your large flat hand slips into mine
  tasting of suncream
will I tease you
            until we kiss?

**Maria Jastrzębska**
**Gorse Track**

When I was your age
my best friend whispered she'd been told
not to be friends with me I was told
the same about you! I yelled
Poppies towered in the sun We tracked
adders, combed dirt for dog-ends, coins
                                        No one
could outrun us We slacklined
rotten planks, vaulted collapsed walls
Streams glittered, mirror
signalling for us to wade, skim
grey green stones
                                        No one
knew where to find us A disused
boathouse, an air raid shelter,
ruins under nettles, grasses,
a flinty track through gorse
were all the future we wanted

**Kate Foley**
**Fresh**

'You wouldn't want
to do anything
*unfresh*'

said Mother Walsingham,
as she separated me
and my best friend.

What did she *mean?*
'Unfresh?'
Took me a long time

to learn
the freshest thing
in life

is to lie
in your woman's
arms

learning
love.

**John McCullough**
**Abracadabra!**

you say, flourishing a chocolate muffin.
The incantation's Aramaic – *I create as I speak* –
and we do, building a new cosmos by the bakery window
with its cheery horde of Chelsea buns, turning our table
into a fairground where I bump into saucers
and make tea dance, replay the Greatest Hits
of my incompetence and cause a chuckle
by saying *implement* instead of *knife*
because it's March and we're ready to throw away
the cold, gobble pancakes with no syrup of guilt
and meet escape artists that locked themselves in buds
and we begin conjuring forsythia from our mouths,
wisteria from armpits and whatever date
spring's cabaret officially starts, we're a sword
some vast artist has already swallowed –

**Aoife Mannix**
**Heading Out**

Broken piano keys crashing against the coast.
The road whispers west where the selkie
lose their skins and you can taste the salt in the air,
the longing for change electrocuting your tongue.
You are breathing fire as you tattoo the last
of the evening onto a storm cloud.

For so long you were crawling
across broken glass, petrified of the vowels
inside your own name. You kept missing
the steps in a dance everyone else
could speak fluently, but you were out
of tune, screeching, tumbling
into crescendos of confusion.

But now, at last, you're learning to swim
through these long nights
when the moon opens up the lake
to lost cities. You are arriving
after midnight, bursting with prayers
all the way from Atlantis to let them know
they no longer have to walk on knives.

Not now, not ever. You are the gospel
in the wind, the shipping news
crackling on a radio in a small town
where a boy girl is slicing
their loneliness into thin strips of skin.
The blood pauses because your voice
smells of the ocean.

**Dean Atta**
**Hip Hop Line Dancing in Dallas**

Outside this club
we may not recognise each other, but

after the Beyoncé drag act,
it's time for the hip hop line dance.

'This club is so Texan, so Black,
so queer!' I think. Me? A Black British man.

I've never heard this song before,
I've never done this dance before,

yet here I am, one of you
for three to five minutes. I'm gently

guided back when I step off beat,
hands take me by the waist or shoulders.

Strangers yet family, wanting me to stay
in this moment.

**Becky Brookfield**
**Moon**

I want the moon in my sky to wane over my lips.
The sharp sliver – a Langston Winter – steps
out of its clouds. I want that ghostly light
to pick out my pikes and ridges – ribs and hips.

Give me a double like Tatooine or Dune.
Give me shape by shadow and shade –
two burning eyes running low in the desert
watching my horizon. Full blood moon.

Our impacts are craters, the sea of tranquillity –
our minefield. Craving her to anchor in me. A Lycan-
like quiver, the earth illuminated, my night heart
waxes, spilling her silver all over me.

**Laurie B.**
**First**

he closed the window
and lowered the blind
so that
the bustle of the market
became a murmur
and the sunlight pooled on the parquet
a promise.

**Vron McIntyre**
**Dirty Dykes**

In *The Guardian*, earnest
dressed sensibly in woolly hats
hanging baby clothing on the fence.

In the *Daily Mail*, unbathed
subversive, paid by foreign gold
dirty dykes carousing in the mud.

Oh, how we love being dirty dykes
proclaim it on a van, write songs about
all the grubby Greenham fun we're having.

**Lawrence Wilson**
**Living**

Music on the stereo – Ella Fitzgerald
dinner dishes, pots and pans – washed
with every quarter hour there are fewer
headlights crossing the Marsh. Dark

and quiet. Clouded over. No stars
no moon, and the temperature dropping
we won't have snow – some towns might
but for us, just a thick, clinging chill

that sort of night. We saw some friends
earlier, drank and laughed, walked home
for an easy dinner, a bit more wine
and now everything settles, calms, quiets

nothing special to share with you tonight
any insights gentle, soft, breathy ones
we are home, we are safe, and fed, sated
the horizon dark – the house candlelit

our hearts are lit, too
perhaps their glow lighthouses the Marsh
you would be welcome here, you know
a drink, a meal – come. Share, sing, live

**Elizabeth Gibson**
**Coming-home Jeans**

These are my coming-home jeans, I knew right away –
or rather, I knew once I'd taken them off for the first time
and never wanted to again. They were smaller, I'm always

in-between, the next size too big. The voice of my mother
told me to stop being silly and wear the bigger ones.
The coming-home jeans knew I would never leave them.

These are jeans made for men but chosen by people like me.
I so long saw them as a blue dragon in the distance
that I couldn't ever have, I knew envy when I knew dykes

in jeans, straight legs, belts, hooks for thumbs, brass studs
you want to taste, metallic like blood. I feel so fragile
when they are away washing or drying. Jeans take so long

drying, and their chemical smell floats over everything.
I wore them to visit my family and, for the hour on the bus,
maybe I made a statement to the lads calling each other slurs,

or maybe they didn't see. But I read my book, felt like who
I was meant to be, in the top-front seat in my jacket and jeans,
through the fairy-lit towns of the North, all the way home.

**Garnett 'Ratte' Frost**
**Time Warp**

Pearls played with

            Genders jumbled
Raising more than eyebrows

High heels
            Ladder the stockings of section 28
Greeting normality

            With a pelvic thrust
Deconstruct me
            Instruct me
Bring out my boldness

Rose tint my world
  With feather rainbows
Kindle my queerness

            Oh Janet
You fucked Frank first
            Oh Brad

Y-fronts? Just            Why?
            O'Brien

I owe you

**Khakan Qureshi, BEM**
## How We Love

How I crave
your hot kiss,
your tongue
entwined with mine
the warmth
of your hand
caresses.
How we lie
side by side
spooning
comforting
relaxing.
How I feel you
miss you
wrap my arms
around you.
How I breathe you
touch you
embrace you
think about you…
How I want you.
How we sleep
we share
we love.

**Lydia Fulleylove**
**Instead of a Bible**

Last week, in Pinks café, I found a copy of *The Well of Loneliness* on the shelf of books for borrowing. And back: the eighties, and us, just beginning, still thinking we were straight women, who happened to have fallen in love with another woman, teachers to boot, the climate hostile, Section 28, AIDS and all that. It was our first holiday together, October half term, and we washed up at Kavos, a half-built villa up the hill in the trees. We caught a bus to Paleokastritsa and instantly fell in love. We climbed the hill to the monastery, we swam in the rocky cove and when it came to time to catch the bus, I, whom you had said never made a decision about anything, suggested, 'Let's stay here. We won't go back till the end of the week.' All we had was a visa card, loose change, towels, sweatshirts in a backpack, but so what. By a fluke – the taverna by the beach had a twin room available, overlooking the sea. 'Here's your key.' Between the two narrow beds, ready to be shifted together and un-shifted in the morning, was a small cabinet and when I opened the drawer, expecting perhaps a Bible, there it lay, bent and battered, ready for sand-sifting hours of reading:

*The Well of Loneliness*

the words    not a warning

but a greeting.

**Joy Howard**
## Don't

don't
tease you    no    okay
don't make you laugh    I'll try
or touch you    well
all right

don't love you
you    with the honeysuckle
in your hair
sweet    impossible

**Annie Kerr**
**Her Blue Shirt**

I want her to shake me out,
snap me taut,
stretch my creased shoulders towards
the tight clip
of pegs on the line.

I will wrestle with a cool breeze
through a morning of unseasonal sun,
reminders of damp sails
and seaside swimming towels blowing
free from sand.

As I dry, my arms reach
to fill with the shape of her
and my back brims
with all this new day
will hold.

Crisp against my collar,
the broad knot of her favourite tie, the
one patterned like dragonfly wing,
like shadows on sunlit ponds,
like quartz on the riverbed.

**Aoife Mannix**
## After the Parade

What can be said by curling one body
into another? The tenderness
of a slow song, the hunger
for gypsy music that still flows
in the blood of wine.
Dance with me, darling,
on this night full of rainbows.
Boys in their leather kisses.
The defiance of fireworks
exploding through the streets.

All those police raids
tossed over for the queer joy
of shaking hips, feather boas.
Rubies and emeralds,
a trick of the light
snatching your breath away.

**Lydia Fulleylove**

## Onion

*for Izzy*

never an onion
like the one we scrumped

as we came down
from the mountain

chilled after a night's wild-camp
in unwelcoming Catalonia

where bars were shut
and mouths closed  tight

a white Spanish onion
splitting its papery skin

we squatted on a rock
facing each other

you tore a chunk of bread
I rooted out the knife

ring-sliced
cool moons

breaking fast
solid comfort in stomachs

we licked our fingers
I wiped the knife on your shirt

in the next field

there were apples

**Jeremy Dixon**
## While Cruising Cardiff Bay

I spy
DAME SHIRLEY BASSEY

schumphing pink champagne
and I can't maintain myself

YOU'RE FABULOUS!
I scream across the bar

NO, YOU'RE FABULOUS!!!
Dame Shirley screams back

I LOVES YOU SHIRL!
AND I LOVES YOU TOO...

BUT DON'T YOU EVERRR
DARE CALL ME SHIRL AGAIN!!!

**Cherry Potts**
**Dance Free on Hope**

Catch this savage symphony –
still so strange,
these lips –
waking to thirst
say: Yes.

Remember the fire-flood,
the moon-melt flow;
how shadows
leave tide-marks.
Say yes.

Dance free on hope –
chemistry may strike:
live with symmetry,
keep supple with song;
say *yes*.

**Desree**
**Foundation**

The average heartbeat of a woman is
eight beats a minute faster than a man's
and I feel that in the way she loves me.
How her hands cradle my joy like it's a gift,
or her eyes find my truth when I've
hid it in the bricks in our living room.

Once, at the beginning she loved me too much,
and my roots surged into the fibre of the carpet.
She has spent the last four years giving them water.

**Elizabeth Chadwick Pywell**
**In a Meadow a Girl Holds her Friend's Hand**

*lovely day for it* dog walkers fucking everywhere
not each other but strutting by every tree
affable in flat caps leaning *now then girls*

anyway she holds her friend's hand with twisted fingers
& her friend's hand is broad & dry feels like lighting fires
with yesterday's paper feels like burning potential

boy on a bike swerves wildly too close knows what he's doing
*twat* says her friend laughs voice low & full of summer
full of bees cigarettes & beer & one more kiss

*lezzers* he shouts back but he sounds friendly? anyway
anyway in a meadow two girls hold hands
*too much dogshit here* *too many men* *like always*

when they lie down oxeye daisies & yorkshire fog against her neck
poppies in her armpits her friend presses against her presses
breath into her lungs *lezzers* she whispers *lovely day for it*

**Sophia Blackwell**
## First Night, New Town
*after Rosamund Taylor*

We climb the stairs.
Edinburgh's rows and ginnels
beckon us up. Town squares are branded orange.

(Who thought Aperol would be a thing?
Stained-glass flame, the aftertaste of polish.
Might be the only drink I couldn't finish).

Tonight we are so stupidly in luck
we'd tell you that first brick was thrown for us.
The abseiling in Parliament? That too.

Thirty years of hurt is nothing new,
and brought me you, and that's more than enough.
And we are this and all of this is us,

and they won't burn our house down (probably)
or cross our names out (almost certainly)
and, if we're spared, I'm yours and you are mine –

as for tonight, it's New Town, pizza, wine.
You look in a jeweller's window.
It's only a matter of time.

**Jane Aldous**
**Old Flip-Phone Videos**

Remember when videos on our phones were new
and I made silly films of us    on the beach
at Achmelvich and Sanna    and west coast breezes
gusted through the microphone as if they were hurricanes
   and that time I kept the Record button on
put the phone between us as we chatted    one afternoon
in the garden overlooking Little Loch Broom
I know which cubby hole my phone's in    with all the other
dead devices    I could charge it up    watch and listen
   there'll come a day when our voices
will no longer be heard    retrieved    recalled
but in those small files on an old phone we exist
the daftness    fondness    two of us    with no wish
to be anywhere else and no idea what comes next

**Jeremy Dixon**

## JOY//US

pink doesn't always suit
rainbows are scarce
unicorns rarer

no permissions required
to share your joy
so share our joy

OUR GAIETY